THE OUTSIDE THE BOX EXECUTIVE

RICHARD LINDENMUTH

authorHOUSE®

AuthorHouse™
1663 Liberty Drive
Bloomington, IN 47403
www.authorhouse.com
Phone: 1 (800) 839-8640

Published by AuthorHouse 05/12/2017

ISBN: 978-1-5246-9150-9 (sc)
ISBN: 978-1-5246-9148-6 (hc)
ISBN: 978-1-5246-9149-3 (e)

Library of Congress Control Number: 2017907229

Print information available on the last page.

CONTENTS

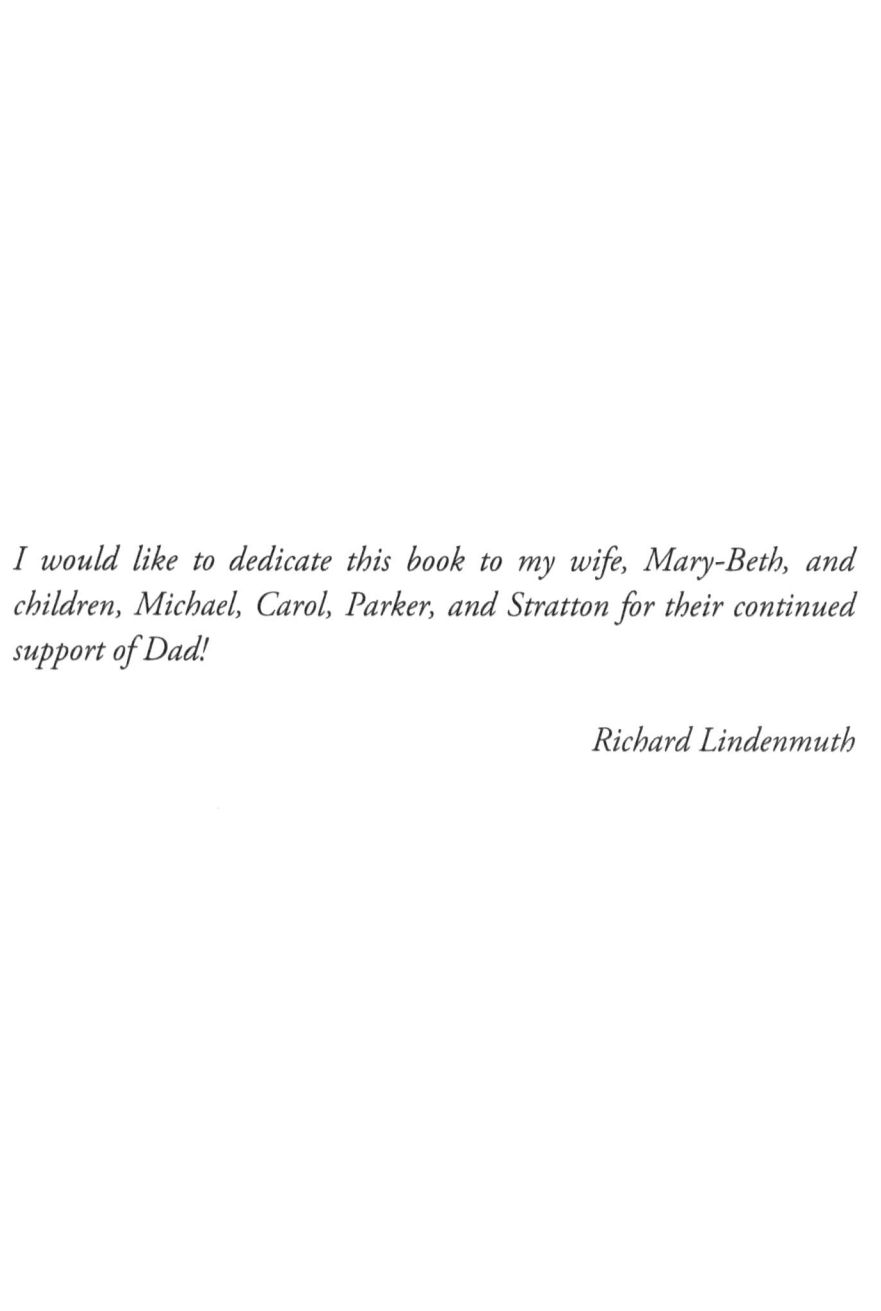

I would like to dedicate this book to my wife, Mary-Beth, and children, Michael, Carol, Parker, and Stratton for their continued support of Dad!

Richard Lindenmuth

REVIEWS

"I worked with Richard and the process he describes works in the real world."

~ Wayne Shortridge, Business/Workout Lawyer, Lead Director, Sanmina Corporation

"An insightful and beneficial read for Interim Executives seeking to master their roles. Thanks, Richard, for sharing your insights as a 'been there done that' leader who walks the talk."

~C S "Bud" Kulesza CMA CFM, Leadership Expert, Dean Emeritus IMA Leadership Academy

"Richard Lindenmuth has held senior executive positions and is consistently recognized for his leadership, strategy development, and execution. He has an outstanding, proven skill set in turning around companies and making them successful. His book clearly outlines the process and how to be a successful Interim Executive. This is a role where Richard has excelled and achieved great success."

~Robert LoPresto, Managing Partner, Duran Human Capital Partners, over 40-year career in senior executive search management

"The business world is always changing. One of the most recent changes is the emergence of the Interim Executive as an effective way to turn around companies or help with mergers. Since this is a new emergence, there is very little information out there about what an Interim is or how to become one. That is where Richard Lindenmuth and his book *The Outside the Box Executive* come into play. His book is the perfect one-stop-shop for anyone looking into how to become an Interim Executive. As a thought leader in Corporate Turnarounds, I can say that Richard is spot on with his information on how useful an Interim Executive can be in the corporate world."

~Dr. Donald Bibeault, PhD, a founder of the Turnaround Management Association, Lifetime Certified Turnaround Professional, and Author of Corporate Turnaround: How Managers make Winners out of Losers

"Good management practices are never interim, and Richard's book is the go-to guide."

~J.P. (Tim) Dolman, retired Vice President ESPN, former Board member, Quantegy, Inc., former Adjunct Professor, Salve Regina University

Nine Steps for Interim Executive Success

1. Active Listening
2. Develop a "shared vision" for the company
3. Be a visible part of the corporation at all levels
4. Recognize and reward success on the spot
5. Understand failure is part of success
6. Think Big
7. Lead
8. Focus on results
9. Deliver the goods

PREFACE

"While interim management is not yet a household phrase, some companies are already getting the best of both worlds: temporary and expert." ––Robert Jordan

There are several unique aspects to the role of an Interim Executive. First, the term "interim" refers only to the time frame and not the actions required. Second, if someone does assign a time frame, it is much like a troop withdrawal: people will sit back and wait until the next Interim Executive arrives. Third, this is a focused and action-oriented role, not consulting and report writing––and there are no such things as "interim" actions.

I want to add a thank you to the Association of Interim Executives, Bob Jordan and Olivia Wolak. They have established an organization that provides a forum and support for this growing American role. An individual cannot join this organization without providing valid credentials and demonstrating success in the role of an Interim Executive.

Section 1

ACTION

"You do not lead by hitting people over the head—— that's assault not leadership."——Dwight Eisenhower

You have now been appointed Interim CEO, CFO, CMO, or CLO. Great! Title does not qualify anyone to lead, direct, manage, or take charge of an organization. What do you do?

You will quickly discover that 80% of the resources, energy, ideas, and experience required for the success of your "mission" sit across the table from you. You must develop the trust of these individuals in order to take them where they want to go.

If you introduce yourself as the expert who knows it all to an already apprehensive management team, you may increase the chance that they will resist even good ideas!

The very first action for an Interim Executive is to listen––and listen carefully. Adding value in a short period of time is your goal. There are many names for the listening process (for example, Tom Peters referred to it as "management by walking around"), and they all result in developing a process for decision-making and developing trust.

The Vice Presidents are the first line of management, and they are important; however, they are generally defensive and sometimes find it difficult to understand how an Interim Executive can come in and tell them what to do when they have years of experience in the company. This is human nature and not unreasonable; however, it is not helpful.

The Tier 2 and Tier 3 people are the keys to success. The Vice Presidents will help you to identify the outstanding individuals in their departments. Discussions with these people will then identify their "go-to" individuals in each area, and so on. If you are listening, you will become part of the culture and less of a threat to the people.

Listening is continuous. It does not stop because you believe that you have the answers. Start to develop areas of focus for the discussions.

Ask one of the key marketing individuals to develop a list of customers organized by revenue (or margin––or both) from the largest revenue customer down to where 75% to 80% of the revenues are listed. In a large, multi-product, broad market company, this approach needs to be refined and segmented in order for the data to become meaningful.

Ask another marketing expert to do the same thing for the products by revenue and margin contribution.

The expectation is that a modest number (Pareto's rule of 80/20 usually works) of the customers/products will represent the majority of the revenue/margin. How does the company make money? This is a reasonable question, and yet few executives can provide an informed response.

Have the individuals share some of this information with everyone. This brings focus to the listening process. "You mean only 20% of our products provide most of the revenue and margin?" "That product has been around forever. I thought it was profitable." This usually leads to other questions, such as, "What about this product/customer?"

Do the same thing in engineering, product development, manufacturing, and all other departments. This includes Human Resources. HR knows that a small group of employees call in sick more frequently than other employees, a small group of individuals are working two jobs and supporting a number of children, and other interesting information about the workforce that will aid in determining priorities if a lay-off is required.

Everything that you do expands the curiosity of the people and demonstrates that you are interested in what is going on in their world.

Active listening is defined in Wikipedia as "a communication technique that requires the listener to feed back what they hear to the speaker, by way of re-stating or paraphrasing what they have heard in their own words, to confirm what they have heard and moreover, to confirm the understanding of both parties."

It seems simple and it is; however, in a community such as a company, individuals will have variations in understanding or communication style (sometimes slight, but not always) about the same issues or topics. The good news is that the knowledge base inside of a company does not usually contain wild variations of opinion regarding the company itself, its products, markets, manufacturing, etc.

The basic rational for listening is to achieve a common understanding between the speaker(s) and listener. It is important to restate issues and responses several times in several ways to make sure that you are on common ground.

In the case of a company, you may talk with several people and find that you need to get them in the same room and discuss the issues to make sure that the understanding developed is really a shared understanding.

There is no room for interpretations or assumptions that lead everyone in different directions. The simple act of restating several times what you heard in different ways assures that everyone is on the same page.

LISTENING IS CRITICAL. NOW WHAT ARE YOU GOING TO DO?

Retaining, remembering, and being able to restate what you have learned is important. Write it down. Identify the individuals who champion this perspective as well as those who may not agree.

Inevitably, you will meet an individual or team that is right on the mark with your direction(s). Use this team and their process to your advantage. Recognize them. Reward them. Work with them more often.

Remember that adding value is your objective. Listening is a gentle approach to establishing a solid understanding of where the organization stands on key issues and what the organization believes is important.

Action is critical. Listening provides data and eventually valuable information about individuals, products, customers, and the organization. Listening is the critical first step in the development of a solid process for decision-making. Report writing is for consultants. Executives act, implement, and execute!

Challenging the ways in which decisions are currently made does not add value. Instead, consider yourself the designer of the new decision-making process rather than the decision-maker. Create a discussion forum where people feel free to speak up. Discuss what people think works and what they believe does not work and why. Let people know that uncertainty is challenging and that no one has the perfect answer.

The leader of today is open to feedback and focuses on communication, collaboration, and coordination!

The best listening and analysis of issues, opportunities, challenges, and current directions is useless unless there is a solid decision-making process that includes communications with the employee population and recognition for the individuals who have provided major contributions to the process.

SECTION 2

DECISION-MAKING

There will be decisions that can be made quickly. The general rule for these quick decisions is that they should be directionally correct and include the ability to fine-tune or even reverse them without any major negatives. The real strategic decisions require a clear and visible process.

It is rare that an experienced executive is going to be confronted with an idea, issue, problem, or opportunity that he has never before seen in one form or another at some point in his career. This is a major value that an Interim Executive brings to the table.

The listening process has provided information and identified leadership-caliber individuals across the organization. It is now time to put this all together in a way that allows everyone to participate in the process. In large organizations, this means at least one or more representatives from each area are invited to listen or present their information and ideas. Subsidiaries and divisions should be treated as individual entities unless they are a functional (manufacturing) entity.

This is a point where the Interim Executive's experience is important. The statement, "If you are not confused, you are not paying attention" (Tom Peters) is fitting. Experience gives the Interim Executive comfort in the knowledge that all this data eventually becomes information and then, through the decision-making process, becomes actionable.

This is not an opportunity for the Interim Executive to "tell" everyone what is going to be done. This is the opportunity for individuals to present key information to their peers and to identify areas of uncertainty or concern. This can include customer/ product line analysis, inventory analysis––particularly slow moving inventory––receivables, critical vendors, quality control, and customer support.

The Vice Presidents do not do the presentations. Vice Presidents have moved up the hierarchy to a position where it is very difficult to admit that they do not have an answer or that their judgment is not perfect. They are, however, very valuable in discussing the pros and cons and moving towards a solid actionable decision.

The individuals should be directed to work as a team with someone from accounting and other departments depending on the product, function, or issue. All numbers must be accounting numbers; therefore, a key accounting person should be part of each team (in a small company, this is sometimes the same individual). They are to put everything together without any guidance or direction from above. This should represent the accounting facts along with their team's thoughts, ideas, and concerns.

Everyone is invited to join the meeting, which may be similar to a town hall meeting. The business still has to run; therefore, a representative from each area is required. This includes administrative, shop floor, shipping clerks, and others. After all, everyone has an interest in the direction of his or her organization. Everyone should also have an opportunity to listen and speak their minds and to share their observations when they return to their jobs.

Good ideas and critical thoughts are as likely (or more likely) to come from the 100th person that you ask for ideas as they are from the first few individuals or groups. Do not stop asking just because you think you have the answers.

The role of the Interim Executive is to act as a facilitator for the discussion. The opportunity to provide direction and leadership depends on the success of this open discussion process.

People will not follow a leader unless they know where they are going and they agree with the direction. More importantly, they need to know and agree with their role(s) in the future and to understand that they will be supported in those roles.

The Interim Executive organizes the meeting, sets the agenda, and identifies the individuals who will do the presentations for each area. This may include areas that do not seem critical to the Interim Executive; however, it is the perception of the employees that is important. Pay attention! They have the knowledge and ideas needed for success.

The goal of the meeting is to let everyone "listen" to the information that has been gathered and formatted (such as 20% of our products represent 80% of our revenues) and to have the opportunity to voice their opinions and receive a respectful response for their willingness to speak up.

The Interim Executive (facilitator) asks questions to clarify, expand, or respectfully challenge the information and to ask everyone for their thoughts on the subject under discussion. (It is of no value to have someone, after the meeting, state a view that was not presented and vetted.) He/she then writes down the issues, comments, ideas, and actions that arise out of each presentation/discussion for everyone to remember, comment on, and/or fine-tune. This is done as the discussion takes place so that everyone can see and comment on each issue in front of their colleagues.

I prefer to write on several easels so that the paper documents can eventually be moved and grouped with other similar comments, ideas, and actions. The walls of the meeting room will generally be filled with poster-size documents. This gives people the opportunity to continue to comment on, debate, and fine-tune all of the areas of discussion rather than just moving on and closing the discussion of any issue.

The facilitator has the responsibility to provide an opportunity for anyone and everyone who wants to contribute. In a large group, it is rare to find those who do not want to make a positive contribution. This is their organization, their culture, and their future––they want to be part of the team!

Listening has provided the Interim Executive with some insights regarding the individual personalities of the team members, so that those who might be more reluctant to voice their opinions are also heard. In addition, the "undecided" are encouraged to become more involved rather than waiting to see which direction is set.

The Interim Executive recognizes that even if he/she has solved these issues in other organizations, the role of facilitator does not permit him/her to provide solutions other than to offer some thoughts similar to "Okay, we seem to have defined the issue. Now what do we do? What alternatives are available? Could we do both? Does anyone have a different view or perspective? I do not want to hear comments tomorrow or next week that should have been shared at this team gathering. What about you, Mr. Undecided?"

After the presentations/discussions on Customers, Products, New Product Development, Manufacturing, Suppliers, Inventories, Receivables, and other core issues, it is time for the facilitator to place the information into meaningful groups and to establish priorities for actions and resources. This is not a forum for all final decisions on all of the issues and opportunities presented. Some areas may need further research and definition. However, you cannot leave the meeting with everyone wondering, "What is going to be done?"

When the individuals return to their posts, they need to be able to say, "This is what was discussed, and this is what we are doing."

Responsibilities can be assigned with dates and milestones so that everyone understands that movement is forward as well as knowing who is responsible for each area.

Further discussions with team leaders and fine-tuning of the missions and timelines can be done in smaller, more focused discussions.

Preparation is critical if these presentations, discussions, debates, questions, and collaboration are to be completed in one day. Organize the format so that presentations require less than 30 minutes, including brief questions, and then provide time for discussions, ideas, and potential alternatives. Work with the presenters on the structure of the presentation (not the content)! Do not focus on solutions too early, or the discussion will go on and on.

RECOGNITION AND REWARDS

An individual may suggest that the "slow moving" inventory issue could be solved by finding a company like Big Lots, Overstock.com, or other non-traditional outlets and getting cash for inventories that are just sitting there. My reaction would be to ask her to gather together the people she believes could help her accomplish that, organize the team, and offer them a percentage of the sale of goods right on the spot (usually keeping the first 50% for the company and then measuring the % against the rest). This provides a visible incentive (not a small one in the case of slow-moving inventory), which shows everyone that good ideas and positive work will be recognized and rewarded!

Do not rush into this particular solution on slow-moving inventory. The first person is likely to suggest a deeper discount on the products through traditional channels. Interim Executives know that the traditional channels, sales force, customers, and support teams are the ones who made this into slow-moving inventory in the first place. They are not likely to do better with a simple discount. Albert Einstein said, "We can't solve problems by using the same kind of thinking we used when we created them."

If that expected response is stated, I simply make the comment that our traditional channels are what made this slow-moving inventory in the first place. Can anyone think of anything outside our traditional areas?

There are several reasons why direction must be provided right there, with participation from everyone. This is where the experience of the Interim Executive provides guidance. The best analysis without support has zero value!

AGREEMENT

This is a time to agree on a big picture of where the company is today. It is the moment to have a solid consensus on those actions that are required to move the company forward. Everyone should evaluate the information and contribute to establishing the direction of the organization. This approach provides ownership for everyone and the understanding that they are all part of the team.

The good news regarding the "big picture" is that almost all of the information discussed can be designated into a few solid categories for action.

- Organization/Communications
- Quality Control Processes
- HR - Safety/Security
- Manufacturing Costs
- Financial Strategy and Controls
- Gross Margin

- Customers - Marketing
- Core Businesses
- Losers - Change Management

Note that none of these categories are verbs.

The objective is to improve corporate performance.

Describe the actions required in each area. Each one of these actions is described by a verb. Eliminate low margin products. Expand the engineering department to include the manufacturing engineering responsibility. Begin LEAN in the XYZ product manufacturing area to establish control and improve quality. Stop sales focus on the "losing" market segment. Eliminate non-core businesses. Raise prices and/or eliminate non-profitable customers. Stop the investment in the product line extension. Eliminate all part-time employees or make them permanent if their job/functions support revenue or margin growth.

Each measure increases revenue, improves cash flow, reduces overhead, and eliminates or reduces expenses. Everyone can see that they contributed (even just by listening and agreeing), and everyone can visualize that "their" company is the kind of place that values their contributions.

THIS IS NOT THE TIME FOR THINKING SMALL

> *"Failure to appreciate the size of profit improvement potential. Many people look for 10 percent improvement levels when overall improvements of 25 to 30 percent can be expected and 60 percent savings in some departments are possible."* ––Dr. Donald Bibeault, *Corporate Turnaround: How Managers Make Winners out of Losers*

My experience is that the quick and easy 10% improvements—such as cutting the travel budget or reducing advertising expenses—last only a short period of time before these same expenses return and even increase.

Interim Executives understand that profit improvement efforts can be very successful if they are systematically organized and executed with clear milestones and responsibilities. They also understand that recognition and rewards for passing these milestones encourage everyone to look for more opportunities!

These actions do not need completed detail action plans today; however, identifying the key individual/team in particular areas, designating the team leader, and asking for an action plan with dates and milestones gets everything focused and lets everyone know that you are now leading the company in the direction that everyone agrees it needs to go and listening to the people who are going to get it there.

PRIORITIES

The process is not complete without determining priorities. The group needs to understand the prioritization. The facilitator needs to provide some perspective. The financial department provides accounting data regarding the cash flow impact of the actions taken, as well as to assess any downside or risk in waiting and/or delaying any action.

I like the direction stated by Dr. Donald Bibeault: "Feed the winners and starve the losers."

Part of the prioritization is identifying those issues and opportunities that have the highest and most immediate impact on cash flow. Other important areas include those that the employees believe are important. The safety of employees, security for the night shift, as well as consideration for those employees working two jobs to support their family are areas that can easily be improved and demonstrate clearly that employees are respected and supported. Actions that are visible and can be taken quickly provide confirmation that things are moving forward.

When everyone returns to their factory, administrative, product development, sales, executive, or admin position, they will carry a very important message. The message is that the "new" person listened to their ideas and is incorporating them into the plan for improving their company.

This shared vision allows ownership at all levels. It minimizes the usual fear, uncertainty, and doubt that come with not being part of the communications process. It develops a willingness to accept change as part of moving forward to improve the company in all areas. Ownership and the willingness to accept change are the two most critical factors in the success of change management and corporate improvement.

The real work has just begun!

Section 3

DETERMINATION

Determination to succeed is important.

It is so easy to believe that the hard work is done; however, after all major actions and directions have been set, with responsibilities assigned to key individuals and teams, the process to improve corporate performance has just begun!

Actions are focused on execution and implementation with dates and milestones. Incentives, recognition, and rewards are expected for success, and support/resources are allocated to ensure the successful execution of the plans.

Momentum

The enthusiasm and support that was developed in the group effort will dissipate in a short period of time unless it is reinforced regularly in a positive way. Many people believe that money is a motivator; however, the best motivation is recognition. When a team hits a major milestone, give them a day off, a team lunch, or dinner with spouses. Raises and bonuses can come later. Money for an individual does not motivate an organization.

The action process is iterative. When a team or a project comes up against a serious unexpected barrier, the objective needs to be altered or even eliminated without blaming the team for failure.

Uncertainty is expected and is difficult to deal with, and an environment should be created to address uncertainty without blame.

As teams move down the path towards executing the objectives, there will be people who no longer agree with the leadership, team leaders who move to another corporation, pregnancy leaves, and other normal issues that need to be addressed. Regular communications, not big meetings, are an important part of the process to keep things fresh and to avoid unnecessary surprises.

Reward and recognize success, but do not punish failure. Failure is an important part of any process. Careful monitoring and communications can minimize the impact of failure in this instance. If the team knows that blame and punishment are not part of the process, they will be quick to point out issues as they arise and not hold back until they become very visible and negative.

Determination also requires an understanding of the occasional "self-doubt." I have never met any leader who is always right. The tough thing about leadership is that if you confess your doubts, you instantly put dents in the trust that you have developed with your Board, management, or employees.

Understand that this is part of the concerns of the Vice Presidents. It is important to have a regular, one-on-one discussion with your C-Level Team (Chief Financial Officer, Chief Marketing Officer, Vice President of Manufacturing, Engineering, Legal, Human Resources/Talent Management) to talk about progress and the areas of uncertainty without increasing stress levels.

Get some distance from the problems before taking any action. Think through your assumptions. Consider the exact opposite action, overcome your short-term emotion, refocus on your core priorities, talk to your spouse, and recognize that uncertainty is part of the process and also part of the reason you are there in the first place. Then rely on the process and renew your determination to make it successful.

DETERMINATION (OR LACK OF DETERMINATION) IS CONTAGIOUS!

If you are determined to make a project successful, and you provide resources and support to the individuals and teams responsible for the success, their resolve and determination will be reinforced. Recognizing even small steps forward and confirming that a step backwards is not a problem also reinforces their determination.

Turn your focus to the Vice Presidents. I usually suggest to them that it is really a "myth" that we are in charge. The reality is that the people actually taking the various actions are in charge. I describe the C-Level group as the "Council of Elders."

It is important to include everyone with functional responsibilities in the "Council of Elders." This includes the Chief Legal Counsel, Vice President of Engineering/R&D, Vice President of Manufacturing, Vice President of Strategic Planning, Director of IT, Chief Operating Officer, and the Vice President of Human Resources. The title of Vice President is not required if they are responsible for a function of the company. In fact, some industry companies have so many Vice Presidents it is difficult to determine who is actually in charge of anything.

The Elder Council provides guidance, support, resources, and even someone with experience who has solved similar problems. We also provide a positive communications vehicle throughout the corporation. Therefore, with this in mind, as the C-Level Executives and "Elder Council," we have the responsibility to be reliable, consistent, and honest in our communications.

Politics start at the top, and it is divisive. It cannot be completely eliminated, but politics can be minimized. Leading open discussions with Tier 2 and 3 management levels (those individuals who report to the Vice Presidents and one tier lower), along with the Vice Presidents make corporate politics diminish. After all, it is the Tier 2 and 3 managers who are often charged with executing and implementing actions. These individuals are product managers, manufacturing supervisors, shipping dock managers, supply chain managers, administrative people, and anyone else who supports C-Level management.

It is politically difficult for a senior person to describe a manager in a negative manner or not include them in discussions if the Interim Executive is reaching out to those same individuals for their opinions. Open and frequent communications keeps discussions on a positive track.

It is important to include every function in the "Council of Elders." I recall an HR executive who did not show up for a council gathering regarding the pricing of the telephone systems that we manufactured. I held the meeting up and asked him to attend. He said that he did not believe that he added any value to pricing discussions. I asked whether he would be involved in the decision process regarding the quality of any new telephone system we purchased for the company and the identification of the number of people who would need to be trained––and therefore the "cost of implementing" a new system. He agreed that he would be involved. I commented, "Your opinion about price is therefore important!"

The Vice Presidents are critical. They have relationships, experience, skills, and knowledge that they have developed over their careers. The process of developing a "shared vision" by listening to the Tier 2 and Tier 3 management and then acting on those comments, ideas, and skills initially isolates the Vice

Presidents. This is why I assure them that as the "Elder Council," all major decisions will be presented for deliberation to the council prior to any final decision. Indeed, their counsel is valuable.

EXPECT CHALLENGES

There is always at least one Vice President who believes that they should have been appointed to the Interim slot. In the case of an Interim CFO, CMO, or CLO, the only difference is that the individual is a controller, brand manager, legal advisor, acquisitions expert, or a person in another visible and critical position. Basically, the individual is someone whose skill level benefits the company in a way that recommends their continued employment. It is easy to identify this individual. It is not always easy to keep them as part of the team.

One example that I will always remember was the CMO (Vice President of Marketing) of a public company that was losing money and at risk for being de-listed from the Stock Exchange.

He was the inside choice to become the CEO. He had a terrific education, ten years as a product manager, and he was eventually an executive with one of the foremost companies in the industry. He was articulate, good looking, and a go-to person for many people in the company. Wow!

The company under the current leadership was losing money. I arrived and completed a deep lay-off within 30 days (no help was offered in identifying the less valuable players by the current team).

An initial meeting, after the lay-off, was called with the Vice Presidents and the Tier 2 and Tier 3 management team. As I started the meeting, Mr. Wow interrupted and said that he could no longer do his job because I had fired some key people upon whom he relied. I could see the heads nod around the table, indicating that Mr. Wow had done a referendum to make sure that he had the agreement and support from the other executives.

What an interesting dilemma! If I agreed publicly, I would have done two things. First, I would have established him as someone who can successfully and publicly challenge the "Captain." Second, I would have had every executive at the table suggesting that they also needed to bring people back to be able to do their jobs.

In this case, I expressed serious concern and said that I was sorry that he could no longer do his job, and that I accepted his resignation. I then asked the Vice President of Human Relations to escort him to the door, provide him with a full paycheck, and establish a time after hours when he could return to clean out his office (with the VP of HR present).

There can only be one Captain. As much as I might have agreed in private and found a way to address the specific issues, a direct public challenge to authority can only have one response, and that is goodbye.

An unexpected result in this case was a very cooperative group of Vice Presidents working to find ways to make the current directions successful and developing new initiatives in similar directions.

Determination to make others successful and sharing that determination with the lead team is a critical aspect of success for an Interim Executive.

The real goal is to add value in a short period of time.

SECTION 4

MEETINGS

Traditionally-run meetings are a waste of time!

Communications require some face-to-face time. Formal meetings, with agendas, are important to that process.

Meetings, at a specified place and time with doughnuts and coffee, waste administrative time as well as management time and do not add value to anything.

Vice Presidents generally tell a CEO what they believe he/she wants to hear. The same can be said for the CFO meeting with his accounting team.

Spontaneous encounters (okay, they are meetings) provide much more value.

The CFO just found out that the bank is going to raise interest rates. A quick encounter with the CEO discussing how to respond to this event provides value. The CMO discovers that the competition is going to lower prices on a key product. A quick encounter with the CFO and CEO leads to a list of alternative reactions that can be reviewed after the short-term emotion dissipates. A brief chat with a shop floor supervisor reveals that lighting is an issue in the final assembly area. An instant response to invest in improved lighting results in better lighting and reinforces the fact that management listens. These encounters have real value!

An encounter in the hallway with one of the team leaders should include two questions: "How are things progressing?" and "Is there anything I can provide to support your efforts?" This has value and does not take time out of anyone's day.

Managers often call meetings to demonstrate their knowledge and to reinforce that they are in command.

I always remember a quote from Margaret Thatcher: "Being powerful is like being a lady. If you have to tell people you are, you aren't!"

Administrative people set a good example. Administrative people include a broad group ranging from secretaries, clerks, inventory managers, payroll people, security guards, and people who clean up the shop floor. They often observe things that others either overlook or would not see with the same perspective.

I have never seen a regular meeting of administrative people called. And yet I watch admin people get things accomplished across all departments, with outside suppliers, working with other admin and support people and generally with a solid determination to do a good job.

What if your administrative people spent their days in meetings? You would discourage that practice! Why encourage some of your more expensive resources to waste time in meetings?

If an executive spends his/her day in meetings "locked" in offices or conference rooms, it does not take long to become out of touch with the day-to-day flow of the organization. It is a waste of time. People believe that the "boss" is too busy for them to get a moment to suggest, discuss, or request something. If your office door is closed and you are not accessible, you cannot listen! Meetings are a waste of time!

Communication, on the other hand, is extremely valuable.

WALK AROUND

Walking through the plant, seeing the housekeeping and workflow, recognizing the woman who is working two jobs to support her family, and talking briefly with the foreman/supervisor about his day provides solid information about manufacturing.

When you take a walk through the shipping dock and inquire how many shipments have been made today and what is our expected shipping level for tomorrow, you quickly have a good picture of sales progress to-date and any production or other issues that are slowing things down. It also encourages others (like the plant manager) to know the answers to these basic questions.

Do not interrupt people from their jobs.

The usual response when an executive comes into an area is to stop and see what he/she wants. When you do this often, it becomes routine, non-threatening, and creates valuable encounters. It also lets the management and Vice Presidents know that it is not very smart to let another executive know more than you do about the current activities, problems, and successes in their departments! Meetings are a waste of time!

BOARD OF DIRECTORS

Board Meetings should not be a waste of time. Directors should do their homework (read the financial statements and the CEO statements of issues and opportunities) prior to the meeting. This allows the meeting to be brief and not just a regurgitation of the financial facts.

Corporate governance requires that a Board be in touch and knowledgeable about company operations and activities.

Board meetings are a great opportunity to have company team leaders present their projects, objectives, and successes to-date.

It provides recognition for the team leader, and it provides the Board with some visibility into the talent pool in the company. The Interim Executive's job is to make sure this meeting is not a waste of time!

I have an MBA (Master of Business Administration), and I work with a number of MBAs. I believe that it should stand for "Master of Business Action." I have never had the time to simply administer!

Lead, take actions, and motivate people. Add value!

SECTION 5

DOCUMENTATION

Write it down or you will forget it!

Actively listening and developing a shared vision for the future is a basic foundation for the Interim Executive. Determination and communications are critical. It is important to write down the vision for the future. It is important to write down the objectives for the corporation and to align those objectives with the team objectives. It is important to write down the plan, milestones, and dates so that everyone agrees and stays focused on the same targets. "It ain't over till the paperwork's done" was a favorite saying of my first boss.

Documentation provides a reference point as programs move forward. It provides a tool to share the directions, tactics, and strategies with key players, investors, and the Board of Directors. The written team documents should align with and be part of the corporate summary.

Part of the value of writing things down is the process of thinking through how to precisely articulate the objectives, milestones, dates, and required resources. The base document has a short life span. It is not a thesis or a consultant's report. It is a part of an iterative process that changes to meet the current requirements. It does not need to "kill a lot of trees."

The "Battle Plan is only good until the first shot is fired" is a comment often heard in the military. Writing the battle plan or documenting the objectives, milestones, resources, and expectations provides a solid base for adapting to any change, positive or negative, that arises in the process of the execution of a plan.

Surprises are the result of not taking the time to document the plan objectives, milestones, resources, and dates along with the internal and external environment. Documentation is also an opportunity to recognize uncertainty. You do not control the external environment; however, the good news is that it does not change rapidly and without signals regarding the direction of change. The buggy whip market did not disappear overnight!

Surprises are not acceptable. The usual reason for a surprise is that someone did not share his/her knowledge, thoughts, and fears about a critical aspect of the plan. I have yet to meet an Interim Executive who is so brilliant that he always asks the perfect question that eliminates all surprises. Therefore, the listening and sharing process includes asking everyone if they are aware of any hidden or potentially negative issues that need to be addressed now.

Again, surprises are not acceptable!

I once heard someone describe a company as a ship. Ships are designed to be out at sea, not hiding in a safe harbor. If the ship is well-maintained, has a good navigator, and the captain pays attention to the weather reports, only a freak incident will sink a ship. In general, management is the cause for the demise of a company!

Documentation also makes sure that other people are not surprised. It clarifies who is responsible, what needs to be accomplished, when it is forecast/expected to be finished, how it aligns with other team efforts, whether it can be done in parallel with other activities, and it identifies those areas that depend on external resources or individuals.

You do not build a large, complex building without a master blueprint supported by individual blueprints of every aspect of the project. Why would anyone attempt to strengthen and focus a company without documentation?

Documentation is also like the music for an orchestra. The leader establishes the rhythm and has the overview, with all critical notes in view. The strings have their notes to play, the brass has theirs, and the woodwinds have their music right in front of them on their music stands.

Together, they combine harmony and solid results. What would that be like without documentation?

It should be clear that documentation is not just a plan. It marks your current status. It shows what needs to be done. It accounts for the recent changes in environment. It provides a tool for communications with others. It provides measurements for quality. It supports training activities for new team members. It provides financial accounting information for costs and taxes. Documentation is a tool to keep projects in sync.

Documentation does not mean sitting in your office writing long reports that eventually end up on the shelf. Today, this means using tools like One Hub, Evernote, and Smartsheet to collaborate on the development of plans, programs, and projects that require solid documentation.

The added advantage is that these tools are similar to and support active listening. If a number of managers are writing down thoughts and objectives in their words, it is easy to develop and to maintain solid "shared" objectives and milestones. I even used Smartsheet to develop a list of potential colleges with my son when he was a senior in High School.

DropBox is another tool. No matter where team members are located, they are able to share documents by simply putting them in DropBox for everyone to see.

It is easy to control access using these tools. Budgets, project plans, customer needs analysis, sales tracking by representatives, and many other useful and informative tools can be stored, organized, shared, and developed on the cloud!

The results of the Interim Executive are measurable––they show up in the financials. The results are part of a process that is expected to continue well past the tenure of the Interim Executive. Documentation is critical to this process.

SECTION 6

DOWNTIME

There are lots of names and sayings for people who work too much: Workaholic, no social life, married to the job, all work and no play make Jack a dull boy––all of these come to mind.

It is important to make certain that you, your C-Level team, and your key team leaders have some balance in their work life. All too often walking around the company after hours you see the same individuals at their desks working hard. Personal questions can be awkward, and sometimes care should be taken not to be invasive of privacy or overly personal when talking with employees. The individual may be a workaholic; however, they may be staying late because they have an abusive spouse or other more personal issues. Everyone has deadlines for projects. Everyone wants to prepare for a big event that takes place the next day. Everyone has something that calls for a little after-hours effort. The critical concern is that these after-hours efforts should not be created by artificial pressure and anxiety in the workplace.

The Interim Executive should set an example with family involvement, after school lacrosse games, band concerts, volunteer community work, or other valuable time away from the office during work hours.

The Interim Executive also understands that after the initial focus on listening, developing a decision-making process with a fair hearing component, instilling the determination for success, communicating the shared vision and individual responsibilities, and documenting everything, the management team needs a break from the constant presence of the Executive. Get out of their hair and let them do the work!

> *"The best executive is the one who has sense enough to pick good men to do what he wants done, and self-restraint to keep from meddling with them while they do it."* --Theodore Roosevelt

Some refer to this as "zooming in and zooming out." Get out of their way and focus efforts on other issues and opportunities along with family, friends, and the vacation that you need.

One short anecdote that reinforces part of this message is a recollection of working long days to return a company to profitability.

In this case, we decided that all of us deserved some time off, so we scheduled several long weekends in a way that allowed everyone planned time off with family but assured that not everyone was on holiday at the same time.

I often work so that I can travel home on Thursday evening or Friday morning (after the positive results of several weeks with long days!). So, I announced to the "Elder Council" that I was going to leave on Friday morning and fly home for the long weekend.

I started out for the airport and realized that I'd forgotten a book that I was going to read on the airplane. I went back to the office to retrieve it. There was not one executive in the office!

In this particular case, I called them at home and suggested that a 1 PM meeting would be great.

We talked about trust and communication at the meeting. We also discussed scheduling time off so that there were always key individuals in the office. Leadership has the responsibility to set a positive example for everyone.

Spend some one-on-one time with your team and key individuals outside of the office during work hours without focusing on work issues.

One other short anecdote. I was announced as the new CEO for a public company that was losing money. On Thursday, I met with the Board and the Vice Presidents and their support people at a conference room in a local hotel. I suggested that since I had a long flight to arrive on Monday, we could have our first detailed discussion at the office at 1:30 PM. I assigned only two items for discussion. First, identify the top ten people in each department. Second, what step or steps do each of you believe could quickly improve our cash flow.

Instead of arriving on Monday, I flew in on Sunday evening. I was at the factory for the shift change on Monday at 5:30 AM. The very first executive to show up was the HR Director at 10:00 AM. I invited him to join me in the conference room and suggested that cell phones should be "stored" with my secretary (who was there at 6 AM!). The last person to arrive at 12:30 PM was the Vice President of Manufacturing.

We concluded at the initial meeting that we would have morning meetings at 7 AM every day until the company returned to positive cash flow.

Six months later, over the Christmas Holidays, the company was cash positive and actually modestly profitable. I invited the team and spouses to a company dinner in a private room at a local upscale restaurant to celebrate. It was a very positive event. It was even more interesting when two of the spouses cornered me and quietly said it was the earliest their husbands had ever gotten up to work!

Getting out of the office

If you are in your office more than 50 percent of every day, whom are you leading and how does that support active listening and communications?

Taking the time to get out of your office and work side-by-side with employees can be an invaluable experience. There are many benefits that you can get from this:

- You get to learn the process of the people who are actually producing the goods and services. This helps you to better understand the end product and how the product or the process might be improved.

- Doing this will help you create a strong bond with your employees, who will feel that their job is important and that you really do care about them. While it is important to have a strong relationship with your management team, it is also very important to have good relationships with those who are actually producing your company's goods. They can also have a perspective that is valuable for process improvement that is different from management.

- This is a great time to network and build relationships with the "unofficial" leaders in the company. Studies have shown (*Good to Great*, by Jim Collins) that the difference between great companies and poor companies is not a lack of ideas. It is whether the ideas make it to the decision-makers/implementers. People with unofficial power (those go-to people who influence other employees but without the title) will often have the best ideas. They are in everyday discussions with broad sectors of employees about their ideas, suggestions, and complaints. These go-to employees will often times have a better pulse on the company than even the HR executive. The only way to identify these individuals is to work with various employee groups and see who takes the lead. Having good relationships with these people (including letting them know that your door is always open) helps you find great ideas and also helps you prevent or get ahead of problems brewing amongst the workers.

- Working side-by-side with your employees allows you to personally recognize their good work. Studies have shown that after a certain wage level (normally around $40,000 to $60,000), increases in wages won't have much effect on job satisfaction and employee retention. Recognition, however, has been shown to greatly increase job satisfaction and employee retention. Working side-by-side with employees allows you to see and give on-the-spot recognition to employees and teams within your company.

One short anecdote... after working on the shop floor for a day, I saw a great deal of material and supply waste. I did not have a way of getting the message to people that the dollar savings for eliminating waste could be added to salaries or recognition dinners. It was near Thanksgiving, so I had one day's waste collected and put into a container. I then took a very large fishing net, filled it with the one day's waste, and hung it on the wall in the employee cafeteria. It included a sign that simply said, "Thanksgiving Turkey for anyone who guesses how many days' waste and scrap this represents, along with the closest guess to how many dollars are represented." The box was filled with responses, so it was clear that everyone was involved.

There was over 80% participation, with no one even coming close to the correct answer.

The real answer, one day's waste and $50,000, surprised everyone.

Several things happened. First, we gave everyone cards that could be redeemed in local stores for a Thanksgiving turkey. We then asked them to think of ways that we could reduce the amount of waste.

The results were terrific. Waste was reduced to less than $10,000 average per day and kept declining!

The management team would never have imagined the innovative and simple methods that resulted from this adventure.

Part of leadership is setting good examples for everyone.

Do not sit in your office!

SECTION 7

ANALYSIS AND FOCUS

Analysis started the day you walked into the office. Listening provided an opportunity to understand the employee's analysis of what they believe is important. It also permitted an evaluation of the key individuals and Vice Presidents. You were able to ask for a list of customers ranked by revenue/gross margin. You asked for similar analytical breakdowns of product lines, work flows, security, IT infrastructure, supply chain, and organization chart(s). You have addressed the big, visible areas, gained the trust of employees, and focused the organization on corporate improvement. Key individuals are doing continual analysis of customers, prices, product performance, and determining where they can add value. What else can be done?

The answer is plenty!

WHAT WOULD A NEW INTERIM EXECUTIVE DO?

Growth can be internal and organic. It can also be external in the form of acquiring products or companies. Only the captain and the executive team have the ability to look out to the horizon to determine whether growth should be organic, external, or a combination of both.

An Interim Executive will bring focus to an organization. Trying to satisfy all customer needs and wants (internal and external) is not profitable. Trying to support all functions and departments equally is not necessary.

The probability that the company is still manufacturing or selling some products that made sense eight years ago but no longer fit your customer demographics is very high. The simple processes that were started a few years ago are already more complex than they need to be. Simple things work well!

Clearly identify the core business strengths and weaknesses. Identify any product, service, investment, or market that is not aligned with the core business. Consider alternatives that might be available to divest product lines or even divisions that are not core to the future of the company. Look at each part of the organization that supports and strengthens core capabilities. Identify any department, asset, or investment that does not support or strengthen core capabilities and get rid of it. Go out, visit customers, and ask them what they think of your company, products, deliveries, and customer support.

Develop a focused strategy based on core strengths. A focused strategy will enable a company to organize and align its structure and resources so that it can grow with a firm foundation. It also identifies anything that is weak or missing, which then leads to a product or company acquisition. A focused strategy creates opportunities for streamlining and simplifying things in almost every area of the company.

A focused strategy is easy to communicate. It is easy for everyone in the company to understand. People at every level can visualize how they add value for the future and understand how to embrace change when it is aligned with core business values and strategies for growth.

A focused strategy is based on the market and customers. It makes sure that the products, services, and customer support are exactly what the target customer wants and needs.

COMPLEXITY

Complexity creeps into any organization that has been in business for a while. The easiest example is to take a manufacturing operation that has grown and added new production lines over a few years.

In this example, raw materials arrive on the dock at a plant. New calibration equipment is added, and since the original space adjacent to the receiving dock is too small, the lab is relocated to the other side of the factory floor. The materials now need to be transported and stored close to the lab, ready for receiving inspection. Once the materials are inspected and calibrated, they are now transported to the "old" storage area, which is located next to the receiving dock where they originally arrived. Some of the materials need to be "kitted" in small containers for initial production. The kitting is done near the inspection station. Therefore, the materials are again transported to the other side of the manufacturing floor. It goes on until the raw materials have traveled around the manufacturing floor many times. It does not take much imagination to understand that this is inefficient and expensive.

LEAN

A LEAN approach will place the receiving, inspection, storage, and kitting all in one place, and the number of jobs dedicated to moving the materials from one place to another will be eliminated. Those employees could be moved into positions of greater value.

We rarely think of LEAN when it comes to the overall business process. A focused strategy permits simplification everywhere. An individual, department, process, or division either supports/ strengthens the core business or it does not. This is a simple but often overlooked concept. The reason is because most people are involved inside the process or are responsible for a small part of the process, whether it is product development, manufacturing, or even IT infrastructure. They do not get to see the whole picture.

An executive has the ability to step back and identify core business strengths and evaluate the current alignment of structure, organization, marketing, and other functions in terms of whether they support and strengthen core business capabilities or not. That is where value can be added. This is a C-Level responsibility. It is a focal point for all executives.

Sometimes it is easy to identify those things that do not belong. In one company that manufactured a variety of high-tech connectors, there were over 10,000 individual products. One product that had been there since the original machine shop days was a bass lure, which was designed and produced by one of the founders for his use and sold to some of his friends, who still occasionally placed orders. The bass lure clearly made no money for the company. We made a final production run and put one in a glass case with a picture of the founder holding a large bass caught using the lure.

It was also easy to identify those products that actually lost money on every sale, and those products that went to only one customer and made only a minor contribution to margin. Sometimes it is easier to start with those products, customers, machines, properties, brochures, and even slogans that no longer clearly fit the business.

Section 8

LEARN

This sounds like something a seasoned executive has already accomplished. Not true! Learning is an ongoing process. It can be challenging, fun, embarrassing, and frustrating all at the same time.

VIEW YOUR CUSTOMERS AS PARTNERS!

Talk with customers frequently. Just like employees, the first few times they really won't know what to share or what you really want to hear. If you do it frequently, it becomes a relationship, and you will learn things that you will not hear from your company team.

Customers will also be able to share their perspectives on your company, the market place, product changes, and other issues that help to influence the strategy for your company.

INSIDE YOUR ORGANIZATION

What about working in the packing and shipping line for a day?

Final assembly requires experience and skills to assure quality. These skills take time to develop, so that is not a smart way for an executive to learn.

Packing the products for shipment to customers, attaching the address labels, sealing the carton, putting a smiley face sticker on it with your initials (if something is wrong, they know who packed it!), and then putting it on the right pallet so that it gets to the correct truck is a lot of work. You learn the process. You learn the way the supervisor operates, and you gain appreciation for your employees. They also appreciate that you took the time and effort to participate.

SOMETHING NEW TO LEARN

Today, social media is an important marketing tool. Google search engines target words and phrases. Take the time to learn the social media process in your company. What are the key words associated with your core business and products? How often do people visit your product page?

Learn how to use Twitter, LinkedIn, Pinterest, RSS feeds, and many other helpful tools for business today.

There are a number of books available on social media. Martin Brossman and Anora McGaha wrote *Social Media for Business*, which I really enjoyed.

It is not just the mechanics for the available tools; it is about links, networking, blogs, following people, associations, and organizations. On Twitter, I follow the National Association of Manufacturing, Freakonomics, Robert Jordan (Association of Interim Execs), Kaihan Krippendorff (expert, author, and speaker on strategy), and others in order to keep up with areas of interest and to understand how these tools are evolving.

Remember that with regard to social media and your company, you are not in charge of conversations. You only participate. It is good to provide some guidelines for your company regarding the use of these tools. We have all gone home and said something like,

"I think I work with a bunch of idiots." It is not productive to have statements like this out in cyberspace.

Learning is important if you want to grow and build your strengths, along with growing the company!

DOMAIN EXPERIENCE

(and other myths)

Domain experience is frequently made a requirement in order for an Interim Executive to be hired or appointed as a CEO, CFO, CRO, CMO, or CLO.

Domain experience means that if you are going to be hired as an Interim Executive in the Construction Industry or Electronics Industry, you must have worked in the Construction Industry/ Electronics Industry and have several years experience in leadership roles.

Review for a moment the various steps and directions described up to this point. Can you think of a company, industry, non-profit, or association where these steps could not be completed and add value without domain experience?

No, is the honest answer! Domain experience is not required.

Domain experience has little place in the world today. If they continue to do things the same way, U.S. healthcare will continue to suffer. Education is one of the least productive areas in the U.S. Teachers probably have some insight into where things work and where they do not. Who will ask and listen to the teachers so that they can begin to develop a system of constant improvement? It will certainly not be those current leaders with tenure.

Domain experience is congested with people who have had the "same" experience in the same environment for a long period of time. A new look from a talented Interim Executive adds real value quickly.

RESUME

A resume is another myth. They are formatted to address a job description that is archaic. The ability to communicate clearly; determination; experience in problem solving; and the ability to learn, adapt, grow, and improve a business are not based on a resume. The value of old tools has diminished to the point where relying on them can actually create more problems.

If the manufacturing plant objective is to hire an individual to run and maintain a specific machine tool, then that is one valid requirement. What are you going to do a year later when technology eliminates the need for that machine tool? The real skill is the ability to learn and provide precision products. It is not to run and maintain a specific machine.

If you are hiring a sales person for the defense sector, it makes sense to hire a person who has relationships in that sector. However, if the experience is in another product domain, is that really an issue?

One question to consider is, "Would your key executives be able and comfortable to act as executives in another industry (outside of their domain)?" The really talented individuals should be able to transfer their communications and problem-solving skills to any domain.

MENTORING

I consider it a part of my job to be a coach and mentor. This helps to fine-tune the "active listening" skill set for me, and it helps me to develop stronger interaction and learning in the company.

If you are looking for a position, it is very important to "find the right boss." This is someone who is a problem solver, wants to advance, has a broad set of interests, solid values, and is someone who listens.

We all have natural skills. Much like an athlete, we study, learn, and then join the field and play the game. Athletes have coaches, so why shouldn't we take advantage of coaching and mentoring as well? Some coaches, a baseball batting coach for example, teach very specific skills. It is important to understand that one mentor or coach cannot provide everything.

I have also found that learning skills does not necessarily mean that they have to be taught by someone in a senior management position. LEAN processes start with the selection of a supplier and follow the materials to the receiving dock, the factory floor, through production, distribution, etc. There are people in each area who have thoughts and skills that can be valuable.

There are financial courses for non-financial managers. Finance and accounting numbers are the language of business, so it makes sense for everyone to have a basic understanding of finance.

The Association for Interim Executives is developing some panel discussions on topics such as "What is an Interim Executive?" There are associations, such as the National Association of Manufacturers, that provide contact and information in specific areas of interest.

Check out the website for the Association for Interim Executives. Look at the biographies of the members. Do you know any of them? Do you have a friend who knows one? Review their websites. They probably have case studies available for descriptions of things that they have done.

The website, www.vertopartners.com, has articles, biographies, and case studies with a blog and a YouTube video describing a great deal of what Interim Executives do every day.

A very big part of any career, including that of an Interim Executive, is working with very solid executives with broad skills. Providing feedback shows that you are learning and clearly understanding the communications. This also develops your listening skills and is very much appreciated by the coach or mentor.

Mentors or coaches are not there to tell you specifically how to do things. I mentor start-up companies, and I would not want to tell them something and have them do anything exactly as I stated. After all, I am not responsible for their Profit & Loss.

Usually a mentor will say something similar to "You are right, but have you thought about this area or consequence of that action? What other actions might be available to you? Can you do both?"

Mentors are valuable; however, you are responsible for your own judgment and actions.

HOW TO FIND A MENTOR

Finding a good mentor is essential in any occupation. It is even more important if you are interested in becoming an Interim Executive. There is a catch-22: Most people will not hire you as an Interim if you do not have experience, and yet you cannot get experience unless someone will hire you.

I actually participated in a course on Mentoring at MIT. It provided some valuable insights.

One way to get around the problem of not being able to get a position as an Interim Executive is to find an Interim Executive mentor and follow them as they do their job. While following a mentor, it is important *not* to contribute unless asked. I have often watched the Japanese method of including a junior person on a project team whose only responsibility is to watch and learn (and maybe get coffee). This process of apprenticeship is common around the world but not in the U.S. This means that there are no programs (yet) allowing you to easily identify mentors. The best way is to take the initiative and ask someone whom you respect and view as an expert in their field. There are many older executives who sincerely want to pass on their knowledge to someone truly interested. It gives them a sense of accomplishment and pride, and it also ensures that their ideas and influence are passed on to the new leaders. Often you can be a quiet participant in project meetings as a learning experience.

One additional thought. I have suggested to young female executives that if they choose to ask someone to act as a mentor, then I suggest a male executive who has at least one daughter. It is surprising how that can make a difference in the active listening and communications process.

You may not know or have contact with an Interim Executive. Select a mentor who is accomplished and well-rounded. There are benefits to choosing one inside the company as well as one outside the company. A retired executive can also be a good choice.

There is a good chance that someone in your family is connected to a solid and knowledgeable executive. Take your time in finding the right person for you, and start slowly. Apprenticeships take time if you are really going to learn something.

Work hard and be a team player. If you establish yourself as a productive member of a team, other members of the organization will seek you out for their teams.

Remember that the reciprocation principle is one of the strongest principles known to man––and one that holds true in all cultures. The principle essentially states that if you help someone, they will help you back––often many times more than you initially helped them.

MERGERS & ACQUISITIONS

History is loaded with failed acquisitions and mergers.

The likelihood that current management has significant experience in acquisitions is very slim.

Mergers & Acquisitions is one of the most complex activities a company can undertake. It is also one of the more important methods of growth in today's fast-paced world.

This is an area where Interim Executives thrive. It calls on all of their skills, beginning with active listening to the thoughts, ideas, and concerns of both the acquiring company and the company being acquired.

The traditional process includes investment bankers evaluating the company and presenting it to the Board and C-Level executives. Bankers describe the company at 30,000 feet and identify the synergies in terms of dollars. They may also consider efficiencies, similar markets/customers, broadening market coverage, and all the other benefits that can be gained. Bankers will also suggest that the acquisition be accretive and add margin and profitability to the financials once the acquisition has been completed.

The companies will have direct discussions. A data room is set up, and the due diligence process is conducted (often without the companies' operating people, who are needed to make the acquisition a success). The Board approves the merger or acquisition, and the transaction is completed.

The CEO, CFO, CMO, and CLO are now responsible for achieving the synergies that have been identified, and bring the synergies (dollars) to the bottom line. They are also expected to open new markets and manufacturing capabilities while they are leading the current company's improvements.

It is rare that the current CEO and management have the experience or bandwidth to complete the integration of a major acquisition.

This is a very good area in which to bring in an Interim Executive. They can work with teams to develop operational plans that make sense to leading this effort. Existing management does not do this every day. They are not prepared to develop and execute a plan to integrate two companies and gain the real synergies available. They also need to focus on their current day-to-day business activities.

The analogy I like is the one where the mountain man says to his camp buddy, "You get the bear, and I'll cook it." You can easily visualize the camp buddy running through the snow with a big grizzly chasing close behind. The camp buddy runs into the cabin with the bear on his heels. He then dives through the back window and yells to his buddy, "Okay, cook it!"

This is often how a CEO and his team feel when the deal is closed, and they are now responsible for integrating ("cooking") the acquisition.

In a Bain study, the researchers state that over 60% of acquisitions fail. They also say that it is common for the CEO to leave within two to three years after a non-successful acquisition.

The first step for the Interim Executive is to meet all of the key Vice Presidents from each company and form two "Elder Councils"––one for each company.

The CEOs of the two companies are not part of the Elder Council. If the CEOs participate in the Elder Council, then they are forced into a position where they are supposed to know the answers rather than having an active discussion on the issues.

The CEO needs to be kept up-to-date. He/she needs to be part of regular discussions. There are times when the CEO needs to listen to the Elder Council present their thoughts and concerns on various issues. The Interim Executive needs to develop trust so that the CEO does not feel left out and appreciates that they are not being put into a position to make every judgment during the integration process.

As is always the case, the most critical people with information and the ability to execute in their own company are the people who report to the VPs and the next tier down.

Identify key individuals. Discuss the integration mission. Identify key concerns. The largest concern is usually, "What is in it for me?" and "Will I have a job when this is over?"

There are differences between coming in as an Interim Executive in a company that is *not* going through a merger/acquisition versus one that is.

The first difference is that the likelihood of everyone in the M&A Company keeping their jobs and the CEO getting the savings and synergies identified for the acquisition are roughly zero. Often, some of the key people required for making the merger/acquisition a success will lose their jobs.

Giving these key executives an incentive to stay and complete the merger/acquisition requires compensation and not just recognition.

In my experience, the best way is to make it very clear to the key team members that they will be given a significant bonus (not just 10% of their salary) for staying around as key members of the team and making the integration a success whether they continue to have a job or not.

This is not just for management. Machine operators need to continue to produce quality goods until the manufacturing process is moved to the new location. If they lose their jobs for any reason after they have stayed to the end and worked hard, they will also be given three to six months continued pay, along with support for job searches and very solid recommendations from senior management.

The threat is always there that if they do not actively participate and do their jobs well, they will be let go before a bonus is paid and severance is available.

These are the individuals and team that will make the merger/acquisition a success (or not). It does no good to have people who are not focused and invested in the success of the project. These are also the individuals who can identify other key team members necessary to the process.

M&A INTEGRATION TEAMS

There are three critical teams in the M&A integration process. The first two teams are formed from key individuals covering all functions in each company. These teams are focused on the issues facing each individual company. There may be sub teams in each company that are focused on special issues. They report to the key team leaders; however, unlike the two teams, the sub teams break up when their special mission is over.

The individual company teams also present their findings, issues, and direction to each company's Elder Council on a regular schedule. The Interim Executive is the facilitator for these meetings and also assures that "side" meetings are not being called by the Elder Councilmen. The Interim Executive cannot be in all places at the same time. He needs a few people with whom he has worked in the past, and therefore trusts, to be his team.

The Vice Presidents are running the day-to-day business. You can bet that they want to know everything. They are, as you might expect, particularly interested in those issues or directions that will affect them personally.

The third team is the "bridge" team. This is initially a very small team with financial accounting, IT, and financial modeling support.

The bridge team will eventually be filled in with key members from the individual company teams once those teams have had a chance to develop their separate thoughts.

The bridge team will be key members of the management and eventually the individuals responsible for leading and executing the operating plan going forward.

It is critical not to try to integrate the bridge team prior to having each individual team develop critical issues, objectives, and ideas that are clearly articulated and ready to be shared and developed into a shared vision. Each team needs to develop their thoughts (using outside guidance) with their own colleagues rather than alongside people with whom they have never worked.

The bridge team is ultimately responsible for bringing everything together in a timely manner. This is easily said. It is based on the work done by each individual team, and then objectives are communicated in a way that allows an operating plan to be developed and executed. Active listening is important, and the Interim Executive is the key facilitator.

This is also the team that goes back to their individual companies and "sells" the results with continued communications and actions that make the direction clear.

Interim Executives prove very valuable in this process. They do not have a narrow agenda, and they actively listen. Unlike consultants, Interim Executives do not write reports. They start in the due diligence process and build a plan with operational teams from both entities. They take on the day-to-day operational leadership roles for a successful integration.

It is surprising how, again with a little guidance, these thoughts, concerns, hopes, and ideas show similarities between the two companies. Each company knows their business, customers, products/services, as well as their strengths and weaknesses.

The bridge team is not just responsible for gathering the information, synthesizing data, and providing reports. They are responsible for developing and communicating the plan that, once approved, will be implemented by them.

There will also be some things that can be done quickly and demonstrate positive actions to everyone watching.

This plan(s) will eventually be reviewed and approved by the Board of Directors. It is important to have the Board involved as the process and plans begin to take shape. This is the responsibility of the CEO; however, the Interim Executive brings everything together in discussions with the CEO first and then ultimately supports the CEO in communications with the Board.

This is where the Interim Executive provides guidance for what I call positive disruption. After all, this is indeed a disruptive process.

The bridge team will work together and be in constant communications with each of the individual company teams. This allows the bridge team to rely on their company colleagues for support in updating information, bringing in other company experts for specific discussions and information, and for continuing the development of a shared vision between the two entities. This is the critical step towards successful integration.

The teams continue in place for the entire integration process and act as the lead operating experts. The integration starts with their abilities to work as the company team and the bridge team to facilitate, lead, and sometimes actually execute the steps leading to full integration.

Interim Executives bring their experience and communications skills to the acquisition process. They do not bring relationships, biases, negative thinking, or fear; instead, they bring the people skills, listening skills, problem-solving skills, and the operating experience necessary for success. Interim Executives focus on results.

Section 11

CHANGE MANAGEMENT

Change is inevitable. It does not matter whether it is the evolution of the basic business model to meet the challenges of today or whether it is the serious fundamental changes required to deal with internal and external problems.

Stagnant or declining revenue, operational inefficiencies, market shifts, and lack of adequate infrastructure for continued growth are all challenges facing companies today.

It is common for current management to continue to try to maintain the current direction and vision. Interim Executives understand that change is required, and they work through the process of developing a new, shared vision for the future.

A circumstance that is unique to the current long recession is that a number of companies have followed the traditional "hunker down" strategies of cutting overhead and expenses, postponing capital expenditures, slowing down product development, and taking comfort that their earnings and cash flow are okay and that many companies are doing the same things.

The length of the current recession and the unwillingness of banks to provide bridge financing for companies in distressed or declining situations has led to serious problems.

Some of the companies have made these traditional changes, and in the ensuing months have lost key individuals and customers, antiquated their production capabilities, and so on, to the point where they need new investment just to get back to where they were prior to cutbacks and delayed capital spending.

Interim Executives understand that simply taking these protective measures without a strategy and plan to keep and even enhance core strengths can result in serious damage to larger companies and self-liquidation in smaller ones.

We have seen large companies disappear in the last decade. Eastman Kodak and Lehman Brothers are just a few of the Fortune 500 companies that no longer exist.

If we look back at the Fortune 500 companies listed since 1975, less than twenty of these companies remain. Some of this is obviously due to mergers and acquisitions and going private as well as bankruptcy. The critical observation is that change is going on in the business world and economy at all times.

What is the financial impact of Obamacare? When will the banks actually start lending money? What is the U.S. going to do with all of the debt? Is it time to bring manufacturing back to the U.S.? How do I find State and Federal incentives or support for moving manufacturing back to the USA? (Especially to my home state, North Carolina?)

ASSESSMENT

Assessing a company's status and ability to manage change is similar to the analogy of the ship captain viewing the weather, current maintenance, and crew training in order to determine that moving to the next port is within the capabilities of the ship.

Interim Executives can provide an assessment of the current company situation in a very short period of time. They can develop alternatives ranging from selling the company to investing in the future and looking for strategic partnerships.

The Interim Executive can develop an operating plan with dates and milestones and then discuss this plan with banks and investors to instill confidence that their investments and loans are under good management.

Interim Executives can ensure that there are strong internal controls and accurate financial information along with leadership to address changes in a pro-active manner.

The assessment is the first step. This is not a 30,000-foot study. It is an operational assessment carefully defining the current financial and operating status of the organization. The assessment is accomplished first by establishing expectations with the Board and interviewing (listening to) people throughout the organization. Current management and leadership capabilities are evaluated in terms of "can they lead their way out of this?"

It makes sense to clearly define where the company is today in order to lead it into the future. An agreed upon financial and operational baseline is required to measure the continued process of moving forward.

It also makes sense to develop several scenarios. I use three scenarios. The first is the pessimistic (worst case) scenario. The second is the "most likely" scenario. The third is the optimistic scenario that includes every positive thing that could possibly happen in a perfect world, which is in every management's optimistic forecast.

The end result of an operational assessment is a clear definition of the actions required to address all issues, along with providing priorities for actions and resource allocations.

We are in the process of providing several examples of operational assessments and outlines for 100-day plans on our website: www.vertopartners.com. It usually takes from 30 to 60 days to provide a detailed written assessment. This includes the very detailed baseline for today. It also includes the three scenarios and the beginnings of a 100-day operations plan.

The difference between this and a normal consulting report is that the assessment includes the outline and first steps of an operational plan, and the Interim Executives are ready to stand shoulder-to-shoulder with management and execute the plan successfully.

The other important difference is that, if during the initial assessment period a need for immediate action is uncovered, the Interim Executive(s) are ready to jump right in and get things done!

PLANS CHANGE

Change is normal. The ability for an organization to adapt and change should be institutionalized. The reason that change management has become more important is that technology, environment, economy, customer shifts, and even regulatory changes have been happening more frequently than they have in the past.

In 1964, 4KB memory took up 64 cubic feet and cost $164. If someone suggested in 1970 that we would have 80 gigs of memory on our desks and have tools like Excel spreadsheets with financial formulae, we would have considered this science fiction.

Today, web-based tools such as Salesforce.com, Dropbox, and One Hub are the norm. Access to information is instant. Certainly most of the company "Googled you" when they learned you were coming on board.

Change is an important part of a company's culture.

SECTION 12

RESULTS

RESULTS ARE WHAT COUNT!

Right from the start, the results should be discussed. Expectations should be discussed. Expectations should be aligned for success. Reasonable expectations are a must. The objective is to exceed expectations, if practical.

An evaluation of the current status is part of the assignment for several reasons. First, initial discussions may be with a Board member, private equity executive, or others who are not involved in the day-to-day operations and are often not fundamentally in touch with the real issues.

The usual discussion is about symptoms or specific areas, such as margins, production costs, the need for new products, and so on.

Most companies, which have been running in the same market for three years or more, follow a somewhat unstructured approach to address these issues.

Often, the measurements are purely financial and do not take into consideration external market changes, new production technology, or other game changers.

Second, establishing a baseline with financial accounting numbers that include a market evaluation, management evaluation, product review, strength (or erosion) of core business, and a definitive plan with timeline and milestones minimizes the difference in expectations. This structured approach also permits regular measurements and reports moving forward.

If an Interim Executive believes that information is being withheld or that the evaluation/assessment process is not wanted, there is valid reason to turn down the opportunity. There are enough challenges walking in the door without adding to them exponentially by jumping in and finding that there is no way to be successful.

Results can be measured in many ways. Financial/accounting numbers are the normal measurement for corporate improvements. There are companies that are distressed or in trouble. Good results can include avoiding Chapter 11 (bankruptcy).

If it is required, liquidating a company, division, factory, or subsidiary is almost always done better by operating executives than by financial, accounting, and legal experts.

One example: A large aluminum wheel manufacture, which was a major supplier for the automobile industry, was liquidated slowly over a one-year period. That provided enough time and opportunity for our team to hold job fairs and find work for almost every employee. It also provided us with enough time so that we were able to eliminate all inventory, including finished goods, work-in-process (WIP), and raw materials. We actually found wheels that had been used for displays in conference rooms, showcases, executive offices, and product management offices, and we melted them down into pure aluminum ingots. We received almost $500,000 for what would have been overlooked by non-operating individuals as simple scrap. We returned $50 million more than investors' expectations!

Corporate improvement can also move in a number of different directions. The largest U.S. producer of professional recording media (audio, video tapes) had customers such as NASA, where the tape was used in the black boxes for all of the Space Shuttles as well as every recording studio in the U.S. When disk drives and new tools arrived in the market for professional recording, it looked like a repeat of the demise of the buggy whip.

In this case, we evaluated what other products could be produced, which would use the same machinery, chemicals, and processes that were being used today.

It took some time; however, we were able to determine that data tape (DLTIV in particular) could be produced in the same factory using the same equipment with some upgrades and improved quality control.

We formed a strategic partnership with a major producer and seller of DLTIV, and we were in production in a very short period of time.

The interesting part of this is that the total market for all professional recording media was roughly $1 Billion, whereas the market for just DLTIV was over $2 Billion!

MEASUREMENTS

How do you measure the environment where everyone feels more secure and happy going to work at the company? How do you measure improved communications and a serious reduction in turnover? Re-shoring manufacturing and jobs that were sent overseas provide good financial results, but they also provide more jobs in a community. These are the results of active listening, employee involvement, clear strategy, and focused direction.

The Interim Executive paves the way for the permanent CEO and CFO to arrive and put their brand on the future of the company.

The company is renting an expert, hands-on executive with a focus on results.

www.ingramcontent.com/pod-product-compliance
Lightning Source LLC
Chambersburg PA
CBHW030859180526
45163CB00004B/1637